BRITISH RAILWAYS IN COLOUR No.3

A
British Railways
Illlustrated Special
By Graham Onley

Copyright IRWELL PRESS Ltd.,
ISBN 1-903266-06-8
First published
in 2003 by Irwell Press Ltd.,
59A, High Street, Clophill,
Bedfordshire MK45 4BE
Printed by Jetspeed

Cover. **The first few months of 1964 will be remembered by our group for the 'Semis on the Sunday parcels'. Sometime around 10 or 11 o'clock on Sunday mornings, both up and down parcels trains called at Northampton Castle station, frequently headed by Coronation Pacifics. Even though there was something a little distasteful in these stars descending from their firmament to such mundanities, we still made sure we were present. Here a grimy red 46228 DUCHESS OF RUTLAND coasts downhill towards its Northampton stop on Sunday 12 April 1964. Between 46248 on 26 January and my last sightings of 46256 on 10 May of that year, these two trains had produced seven of the survivors for me, 46228, 46235, 46239, 46240, 46245, 46251 and 46254.**

INTRODUCTION

I have always considered myself as lucky as the next person. Whatever calamities have befallen me, they have never seemed, overall, to have outweighed the pleasure provided by the now sadly missed British Railways, even if they did remove the ordinary workaday steam loco from my life a little too early for my liking! Like most of my ilk, I cannot truly remember any of the 'firsts' that we all lay claim to. However I have a myriad of recollections, from gazing awe-struck at an unrebuilt Patriot 'on the shed', possibly in about 1950, through to the last miserable days of the mid-1960s when whole classes, or last survivors of locomotives from all Regions could disappear seemingly overnight, leaving us with those we had most maligned in our early days such as Black 5s, Austerities and B1s. In between, the BR Standards had arrived; many combinations of liveries had finally settled down into BR green and black, supplanted by the unexpected, but very welcome maroon dressing on some ex-LMS Pacifics – if only the BR blue had survived. Not only were there gains, but we lost steadily also, if not spectacularly, pre-Beeching. Stations, lines and services disappeared, so did the last original Royal Scots, the Turbomotive, sloping Coronation smokebox fronts, WINDWARD ISLANDS and 60700 to name but a few.

As I became older, like everyone else I suppose, I came to appreciate that life beyond my immediate boundary also had something to offer. There was the comforting realisation that my interest was producing more than just an encyclopaedic knowledge of the names of just about every loco ever built and shed code ever allocated – I actually knew the location of many towns sooner than I (and many like-minded contemporaries) might have been expected to. During a junior school geography lesson, I did not have the nerve to contradict our teacher who told another lad that Lichfield was not a city, but I was confident that the LMS would never have got it wrong with 6250. I also came to accept that the old LMS was not necessarily any better than the other old railway companies. It was this acceptance, coupled with the dread thought that steam really was going to disappear (in effect) comparatively soon, that turned my thoughts to photographing the passing scene. Doubtless anyone who has ever photographed a railway subject soon realised that it was not easy, it was not cheap and that however many films were exposed, it was not, and never would be enough. That is why I am so thankful that those with the benefit of a few more years than myself did get around more than I did and at an earlier period. That said, I am thankful that I, and my fellow 'squad' members almost adequately covered 'our (small) patch'. I must have spent a small fortune on films during my first years in employment, but the agonies of seeing the scene changing, not for the better from my youthful viewpoint, led to the extravagance of a 25ASA Kodachrome 2 colour film in September 1962, and apart from the odd experiment, I have stuck with it and its successors to this day.

Beyond Far Cotton: 'The Squad'
One of the benefits of being the youngest member of the family was that at an earlier age than might have been expected, I was allowed to go and watch trains in the care of brothers. By the time I was about seven, I was spending most of my non-school time, summer and winter alike, in the club-like atmosphere of the fields adjoining Duston Junction West, Northampton. There was a combination of established, older boys (as old as fifteen!) who were held in awe by the other, younger element of

which I was a part. Everything seemed as safe as houses – it must have been because the kids of Far Cotton were members of this club which also provided for 30-a-side cricket and football games according to the season, as well as other more traditional pursuits such as canal-jumping, tree climbing, and if truth be told, the odd bit of allotment depredation to provide roast spud feasts under the 'bridge' on dark evenings. As those of similar age to me became a little older, we became a 'squad' which varied in size and make up around a core. The main core, which had formed by the mid to late 1950s survives to this day, still managing to discover that even though we may have thought we knew it all, we did not and do not! Rest assured, we are still having fun, thanks to British Railways in general, and to the people who passed our way in those days, whether driving or firing a Jubilee on the 'half past one' or the guard on the veranda of 'another bloody goods' staggering up the 1 in 200 past our base behind an LNWR 0-8-0. I thank them all.

Locomotives present at Northampton shed on Sunday, 15 May 1960
Visitors: 42920 (Stoke), 43034 (Nuneaton), 44235 (Kentish Town), 44860 (Rugby), 44909 (Rugby), 45038 (Monument Lane), 45231 (Aston), 48018 (Rugby), 48124 (Derby), 48173 (Rugby), 48325 (Willesden), 48476 (Willesden), 48600 (Willesden), 90305 (March), 90719 (Canklow – this was the pick of the bunch!), 92024 (Wellingborough), 92108 (Leicester), 92119 (Leicester), 92130 (Toton).
Our lot: 41218, 41219, 41278, 43399,

43957, 44076, 44219, 44242, 44247, 44491, 44524, 45050, 45091, 45307, 47318, 48090, 48147, 48305, 48422, 49105 (withdrawn)
Locomotives present on Good Friday, 16 April 1965
Diesel shunters: 12047 (Rugby), D2907 (Rugby),D3053 (Nuneaton)
Main line diesels: D5010 (Rugby), D5024 (Willesden), D5078 (Willesden), D5079 (Willesden), D8042 (Willesden), D8043 (Willesden)
Steam locos: 48637 (Leicester), 41218, 41219,

44869, 45134, 45302, 45426, 48354 (Stoke), 44936, 45287, 45308, 47286, 47499, 47590, 48020, 48247, 48360, 48493

As young linesiders we felt that any parcels train could provide either an ordinary engine from an unusual shed, or an extraordinary engine from one of the more usual sheds. Frequently of course it was neither of these combinations, and by Sunday 3 May 1964 Willesden Pacific 46239 CITY OF CHESTER came in the third category of a common shed providing an engine we had seen countless times before. Yet in the way of the times we were as pleased as if Bristol Jubilee KEMPENFELT or Perth's KEPPEL of yesteryear had turned up. CITY OF CHESTER is seen coasting downhill from Hunsbury Hill tunnel, past our magical fields, one of which had already been turned into an industrial estate, the other of which would be a housing estate within five years or so. Electrification beckons, and this was my last encounter with 46239.

That the local enthusiast grapevine was stuttering a little became blindingly obvious to me as I blithely cycled to work on the morning of Friday 1 May 1964. As I neared Northampton Castle station, Coronation Pacific 46245 CITY OF LONDON, in immaculate condition, was heaving a lengthy southbound train out of the station. Attempting to contain the shock I realised this was no ordinary Euston commuter train. During the course of the morning I was able to establish that the train involved was an 'old age pensioner' special from the town to Eastbourne for an early holiday break. As the next day was to see hordes of Preston North End supporters travelling to Wembley for the FA cup Final, I felt that all was far from lost. As it happened, Preston were not the only losers on the Saturday – all the special trains passing Roade that day were Stanier class 5 or Britannia hauled, with but one exception. The Midland Pullman was hired to take the Preston club officials to Wembley, making undoubtedly the Pullmans' only revenue earning visit to the west coast main line. Again, we had confidently been told by friends 'in the know' to expect Coronations by the score! I needed a victory, so, independent of the grapevine, reasoning that the pensioners would return the following Friday afternoon, I arranged my working day to suit. As far as I am aware, they have yet to arrive back! This made me 3-0 down, but a late consolation was the very welcome sight of Crewe North Jubilee 45704 LEVIATHAN, running light engine northwards through the station during that afternoon. 45704, celebrated locally for its ex-Kingmoor and ex-Farnley Junction credentials, still retained its properly sited top lamp bracket and, more importantly, its red-backed nameplates, St Rollox style cabside number and Fowler tender. I told myself that my first (and, as it proved, my only photograph of such a Jubilee combination) was more valuable than another shot of a Coronation.

We had seen BR standard class 4 2-6-0s at Northampton; odd members of our squad may have seen a very occasional Sutton Oak engine locally. Yet I would still bet that 76077, passing Northampton No.3 box at Spencer Bridge with a down freight on a very spring-like Friday 17 April 1964 was a first. Visits from March-allocated members of the class, working Peterborough-Northampton services, were not unknown at this time, being invariably in a filthy condition which did not compare to the standard we had come to expect on Eastern Region A4s. I would have to agree that in terms of loco cleaning, the LMR had a bit to learn, so I imagine 76077 had recently visited works or been used on a railtour, though perhaps I do Sutton Oaks cleaners a disservice.

One of our Western Region refugees, 70029 SHOOTING STAR by now gathering layers of Brummie grime in the care of Aston shed, was photographed broadside on waiting for the road at Duston West, with a northbound fitted freight on Tuesday 10 March 1964. Of the erstwhile WR Britannias, I can only recollect that 70021 held onto its smoke deflector handrails, although its escape to a more receptive Trafford Park was not until mid-1958.

Against a background of the products of the late 1950s bus-building industry, a nameless O2 0-4-4T heads south out of the Ryde Esplanade station, passing a train heading for Ryde Pierhead station. From the loss of the nameplates, the time would be during 1965 or 1966. For the majority of 'off-island' enthusiasts, once they had discovered the time-warp of the Isle of Wight, with its Victorian style trains headed by the novelty of small, named tank engines, in delightful scenery, it became part of the badge of office to make the pilgrimage as soon as sufficient funds became available, preferably armed with a camera and copious amounts of film. Photograph Dr A. Roscoe, The Transport Treasury.

An internal user train of ballast makes good progress deep in Southern Region third rail territory, behind a Bulleid Q1 0-6-0. Someone with an eye for nostalgia for an even earlier age has imaginatively replaced some of the layers of grime covering the locos front numberplate with strategic use of chalk, cleverly recreating 33020's original Southern Railway number, C20. Whilst the Q1 class would hardly be a candidate for a beautiful locomotive contest, in the context of handsome was as handsome did, they would be well up the league. In the manner of the times, a March 1965 Railtour brought a combination of U 31639 and Q1 33006 to Northampton, the first visit of SR power to the town since the elderly dodderings of a small number of pre-grouping 4-4-0s, loaned to a probably ungrateful LMS and used on Northampton-Peterborough services for a short time during the war. Photograph Dr A. Roscoe, The Transport Treasury.

Saturday 15 September 1962 was rather overcast, bordering on drizzle, but the scene had to be recorded. This is the west coast main line, looking south, immediately to the north of Blisworth station, closed on 4 January 1960. The former SMJR platforms can be seen on the right, with recently erected canopies. These had been put up on Blisworth's elevation to stand-in mail depot during the upheavals caused by the electrification work then becoming more intensive as the tide rolled southward. A one road engine shed once stood between the Blisworth SMJ signal box and the clearly visible site of the turntable (the grassy area to the right) but it had long disappeared by this time, as had the best days of the 'old smudge' as we irreverently referred to a line having none of the glamour of its neighbour to the left.

The first yellow-striped cabside I noted was on 11 August 1964. Like countless others, I pondered the significance of such an unusual splash of colour only to discover that the stripe was akin to being unclean. The penalty was to be barred from the electrified lines south of Crewe as from 1 September of that watershed year. In the short period from seeing 45567 so disfigured, until Warrington's anonymous 45655 made what was without doubt its last foray south of Crewe on Saturday 29 August with a northbound fitted freight, 45595, 45704 and 45726 presented themselves in the same garb. Interestingly, the same period saw 45583 and 45672 not yet treated. The only be-striped Stanier Pacific to pass across my lens was the very presentably clean 46256 SIR WILLIAM A STANIER, FRS, seen passing over the A43 trunk road north of Blisworth village on the afternoon of Tuesday 25 August 1964, with the up 'Lakes Express'. This particular train remained steam-hauled to 'The End' –generally considered to be 31 August 1964. The Stanier Pacifics of course were soon to disappear from our lives overnight. I sometimes wonder how we coped without the counselling that would have to be made available today.

Sunday 7 October 1962 and clean engines were becoming a bit of a rarity. Nuneaton's 42960 was facing the wrong way, but it had to be recorded. If I was asked today to draw the lining of mixed traffic locos, I doubt that I could – but if I saw the wrong layout, it would be the proverbial sore thumb. Nuneaton locos were not particularly frequent visitors to our patch, nor were Stanier 2-6-0s, except for Sunday 7 January 1962 when, amazingly, Nuneaton's 42954 and 42955 with 42957 of Aston invaded the shed. The real place to see them locally was on the main line proper, usually on parcels trains, when we would pray for a visitor from Mold Junction or Birkenhead, rather than Crewe South

Up until twelve months previously, there had been a possibility that this diverted Sunday morning Euston to Carlisle express would have produced a Coronation Pacific. However, by 20 June 1965, the best in the realms of steam power we could hope for was a Stanier Class 5 4-6-0, or more likely one of the Britannia Pacifics, most of which had by then become domiciled on the West Coast main line from Crewe northwards. How strange that I had managed to choose this excellent vantage point to photograph one of the (then accursed, now lamented) English Electric Type 4 diesels, D229 SAMARIA, seen from the lineside of the direct 'new' route from Northampton to Roade, as it approaches Duston West junction from the Blisworth direction. Electrification was a mere three months away and SAMARIA and its multitude of sisters would soon be finding themselves in the same evaporating north western pond that would dry up for steam over the following three years or so.

An example of just how attractive a real black locomotive can be. 45242 could not have been long out of Crewe Works when it was photographed in alien territory 'on the Western' at Banbury during August 1965. 45242 had been at Edge Hill since at least 1950 and unusually, considering the frequency of LMR transfers, actually managed to survive at that same shed until modernisation finally caught up with it in June 1967. From late 1963/early 1964 Crewe Works was obviously looking for cost cutting wheezes. One highly labour intensive job disappeared overnight with the decision to cease the lining out of locomotives passing through the paint shop. This meant the return of 'black' Black 5s which, while the black remained glossy, looked a treat. It has to be said that unlined green locomotives looked atrocious. Occasional combinations of lined/unlined engine and tender also looked a little incongruous until it all disappeared under the grime. Photograph Jack Kirke, The Transport Treasury.

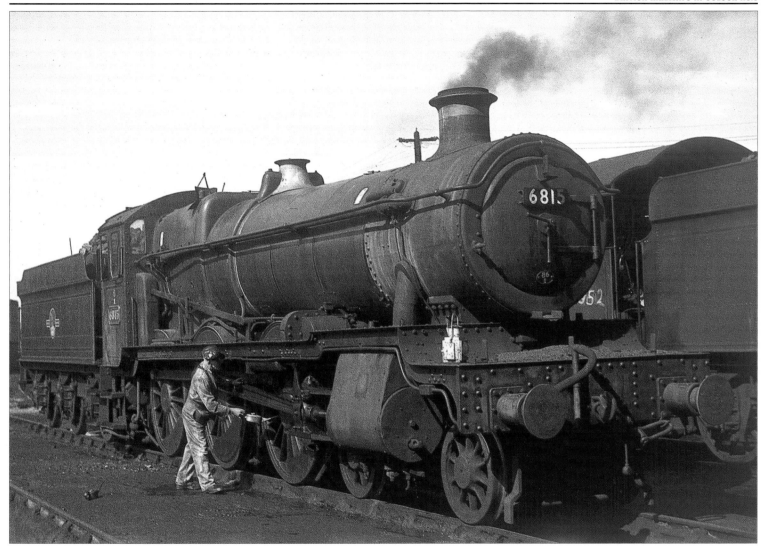

By September 1965 Banbury shed had become part of the London Midland Region. Visiting 6815, formerly FRILFORD GRANGE was, however, well and truly part of the Western Region, allocated (if the shedplate is to be believed) to 86E Severn Tunnel Junction. Such survivors as clung on at that late date in Western Region history rarely retained their nameplates and frequently lost also cabside and smokebox door numberplates, so 6815 could almost be considered well dressed. Photograph Jack Kirke, The Transport Treasury.

The arrival of the first cars amongst the squad elders led us to Kings Sutton, at the southern tip of Northamptonshire early on Saturday 14 September 1963. Our short time there and at Banbury General station produced a little of what we were after. In addition to an immaculate 6979 HELPERLEY HALL standing pilot at the station, 7014 CAERHAYS CASTLE was seen on a southbound express. Lack of a light meter meant that the only decent sunlit (they had to be in those days) shot was of, some might say, the most aptly named Hall, 7915 MERE HALL as the old joke runs, on an up freight. This was the very month that Tyseley, surely forever 84E, was dragged screaming into the LMR, where it was given the hallowed ex-Rugby code of 2A. Who said 'to the victor, the spoils'?

A masterpiece of planning and endurance. Saturday 18 April 1964 required me to be at work between 8.30am and midday. I then needed to be at Midsummer Meadow at 3.00pm for an end of season Northampton Town Football League Division 1 fixture, the result of which would not determine entry into Europe for the following season. In between I had to cycle the twenty miles or so to Culworth, on the then just about still open old Great Central main line. There, if it was running to the times that I had gathered from the none too reliable grapevine, I could expect to see a southbound railtour, headed, if the grapevine was still credible, by the recently preserved A3 Pacific 4472 FLYING SCOTSMAN. It all worked out right, and an acceptable photograph of 'The Great Central Railtour' was obtained as it stormed south past Culworth station signalbox. I was standing on the north end of the island platform of the closed, but still intact station. Courting controversy, dare I say that I still prefer Brunswick to apple green.

On the afternoon of Tuesday 25 February 1964 MALLARD, restored to LNER condition for preservation, was due to be towed south up the Great Central main line to what was then expected to be its permanent home at Clapham Museum of Transport. An afternoon off work was booked, bikes oiled and off we went. Standard Class 5 73045 (a Woodford loco) eventually appeared, towing a tender-first 4468 at about 7pm. Although acceptable slides were obtained, the workaday shots of that afternoon have more appeal. A double chimnied 9F 2-10-0 from York, 92005 stands amid the clutter of a still busy (though no one doubted that it existed on borrowed time) Woodford Halse shed. The smoke haze hanging over the shed on a Sunday afternoon, deep in the rolling Northamptonshire countryside, is an abiding memory – worthy itself of preservation!

If ever I could have confidently forecast a loco's eventual preservation, it would have been the first of the BR Standard Class 5 4-6-0s. I defy anyone to say that they were not highly attractive, as well as, I assume, relatively highly efficient, given their family lineage. My first sighting of these had been during the summer of 1952, when for a few months one of our few regular expresses might frequently have been graced by one of 73025-73029, which had gone new to 24E Blackpool. This train, known to all and sundry as 'the half-past-one' was a notorious cause of lateness in arrivals back for the afternoon sessions of the local Junior school. The excitement engendered by this development softened the blow of the (temporary) absenting of the Blackpool Jubilees. Clearly, by 25 February 1964, 73000, cascaded to a not necessarily willing Woodford Halse had seen its best days. Things were unlikely to get better and 73000 eventually failed the preservation test.

Another of the fruits of the 'Semis on the Parcels' crusade of 1964. On the dismal mid-morning of Sunday 5 April 1964 46235 CITY OF BIRMINGHAM ambles alongside platform 6 at Northampton Castle station with a northbound parcels, which did not on this occasion call for business. 46235 did not, from my recollection, have any cleaner's attention for the rest of its time which ran out, with that of the other survivors, early that autumn. The up platform is occupied by another parcels train; this offered the opportunity of photographing a 'Semi' but an EE Type 4 had presented itself so, hoping for a second chance, I stationed myself on the temporary footbridge which had been installed half way along the main platforms. In the background can be seen West Bridge, devoid of parapets, in the throes of lifting for the coming electrification. There were many times when both the main line and the Northampton loop were subject to Sunday electrification works, and the operators must have wondered if they were ever again likely to get the opportunity to run a proper railway – does this have a modern ring to it?

A2/3 60513 DANTE taking water on Langley troughs in July 1962. As an outsider, it always appeared to me that the A2s were the poor relations of the many Pacifics on the eastern side of the country, well behind the A4, A3 and A1 in the pecking order, although I am certain that they played their part in the overall scheme. I loved the racehorse names of the old LNER. They were so right for speeding steam engines and much more suitable than some of the modern efforts such as 'Rotary International', 'London School of Economics', 'European Community', worthy as each may or may not be. I would not criticise today's 'traditional' names such as 'Durham Cathedral' or 'County of Somerset' and salute whoever decided on 'The Lion of Vienna' but I wonder what intelligence decided to strip the Class 60 diesels of their fine original names based on mountains and heroes of science, to replace them with 'GEFCO' for instance? Photograph Jack Kirke, The Transport Treasury.

The unmistakable stamp of the early 1960s, as E3015 heads south off the Edgeley viaduct and through Stockport Edgeley station. This class, to which many a dyed in the wool steam man may now admit to a little more than just passing nostalgia, provided the first of the modern fleet of electrics which started off services on the Manchester to Crewe section of the London Midland Region modernisation plan. E3015, in the appropriate and attractive 'electric blue' livery, complete with individual cabside numbers and stainless steel modern version of the lion and wheel emblem has yet to gain the all pervading electric flashes and the yellow front lower panel, which can be seen to be disfiguring the electric loco lurking in the background. Photograph Dr A. Roscoe, The Transport Treasury.

The diesels have completed their take-over at Edinburgh Waverley. The southbound 'Flying Scotsman' looks to be about ready for the off behind the Deltic, traditional power since the finish of the summer 1961 service, which saw the end of the A4s on the non-stop between London and Edinburgh. The yellow panels on the Deltic and the EE Type 4 D368 are of differing styles, pre-dating the garish all-over yellow front ends which eventually disfigured all locos. The modern style Thistle headboard dates the picture as after mid-1964. Readers may wish to ponder the identity of the Deltic. I reckon it to be D9010, based on a double line nameplate (a Regiment), therefore a Haymarket unit (not a Kings Cross, and most unlikely a Gateshead example) with a badge above the nameplate. Photograph Dr A. Roscoe, The Transport Treasury.

Our very own, much lamented Ivatt Class 2 41218 stands forlornly banished to the far end of the shed yard at Northampton on Sunday 18 July 1965, its first day of 'laying in state' after withdrawal. 41218 came new and 41219 came almost from new to the shed some time in early 1948 and, in effect, stayed until the end, 41219 going to Leicester in 1965 for its last two months in service. At that time we had not known life without these two. My footplating older brother liked them as much as we did, because a day on them was, in his words, like a days holiday! Also seen from the cab are Duston West Junction box, the direct line to Roade, our base alongside the canal and the towpath that led, in the immortal words of the Shed Directory 'to the shed'.

As the dread day of electrification switch-on crept ever nearer, the fare on offer at both Duston West and the greater West Coast Main line included less and less steam. The procession of Sulzer Type 2 and English Electric Type 4s was interspersed with, at best, Stanier Class 5s and 2-8-0s and Standard 9Fs and Britannias, and then in a ratio of something like 5 to 1 in favour of the diesels. In these doom-laden times we took to haunting lesser known railway parts of the town, including the local track maintenance depot. Nearby was, and still is, a cul-de-sac of about twenty houses, built by the LNWR and rejoicing in the name of Claughton Road, a choice of name which we felt was not a coincidence. Lunchtime on Thursday 13 May 1965 found one of our local mascots, Ivatt 2-6-2T 41218, pausing between shunting operations at the depot. By this time only 47590 of our 'native' Jinties was active. The other two, 47286 and 47499, spent most of their time dead on the shed and the use of 41218 was merely another example of cascading, usurping the Jinties from their traditional tasks at the depot while waiting for the inevitable.

By 14 August 1974 steam had been gone from my locality for almost nine years, and once steam had finally disappeared I'd come to realise that even the diesel and electric classes responsible for steam's demise had a finite existence. They too would ultimately slip away. Consequently an excuse was found to forsake the nearby beaches, in favour of a visit to Exeter St David's station. From the platform end could be seen a very presentable Brush Type 4, or Class 47, 47079, complete with its GEORGE JACKSON CHURCHWARD nameplate, stabled in what was the west end of the old Exeter steam shed, coded 83C until its reduction to a mere stabling point during 1973. 47079 had started life in 1965 as D1664, allocated to 87E Landore. With the continuous re-numbering of this once vast class, I really have no idea if it exists today in another guise!

1.45pm on Tuesday 14 April 1964 sees, most unusually, a long rake of iron ore empties heading south past Duston West signalbox towards Blisworth, and the main line, where Jubilee 4-6-0 45586 MYSORE of Crewe South shed would have to wait its turn to get out onto the main line. There was a period during the summer of 1955 when 45586, then towing a Fowler tender, had been allocated to Bushbury shed, and there is no doubt that I had stood in that same spot more than once to watch it roar past with the regular Wolverhampton to Euston train which paused at Northampton Castle station at around 11.30am. Note the early arrival of electrification paraphernalia on the line passing over the train, also the underbridge to the right of the signalbox, under which passed a local ironstone line, closed well before my time, but whose concreted-over tracks had become visible once more some half a mile behind the camera as the concrete deteriorated. The grass-covered ground to the right of the new fence was still as it had been left when this section of track had been lifted, and it used to provide interesting cycling challenges for generations of Far Cotton children between trains.

A smart permanent way train idles in a short siding opposite Bletchley No.2 box, immediately north of the station. Bletchley's 8F 48154 looks surprisingly quiet, and is devoid of headlamps. In earlier times the presence of such a train, ready for the off would have been a clear indication of a Sunday picture, but by the date of this photograph, September 1962, such workings often scuttled into action between trains. 48154 will not be going far for a while, with a down main line train signalled by the massive 'repeater' pegs, long a Bletchley landmark, although all is quiet in the up direction. What looks to be a Jinty is stored at the end of the same siding. Photograph Jack Kirke, The Transport Treasury.

Another year or so to go before Jubilee 45593 KOLHAPUR heads for the Midland Division and fame and immortality through the sanctuary that was Leeds Holbeck for so many of the class. KOLHAPUR looked more presentable than we had come to expect by the relatively late date of September 1962. The fireman takes a breather as the Jubilee coasts southwards at Bletchley with a Euston bound express of at least ten coaches, bearing the then relatively new type of reporting number, in this case 1A42. September 1962 saw the end of the Summer Timetable and with it went the last real opportunity to see main line steam in any volume on the west coast main line – whatever came in the following years was, in truth, the scrapings from the table. Photograph Jack Kirke, The Transport Treasury.

An hour spent on an overbridge near Werrington junction, north of Peterborough, straddling what had become a three track east coast main line epitomised another stage of progress. Three northbound expresses passed on a beautiful June 1978 morning. The first was headed by one of the Class 47 diesels of the 47401 series, which, as D1500 onwards, late in 1962, heralded the arrival of the modern A3 equivalent. The second was one of the then recently arrived HSTs. The third was this immaculate, but unidentified Deltic of the old North Eastern or Scottish Region regiment series – clearly the latter-day A4 equivalent. To be fair to the HSTs, at some 5,000hp they are in a class of their own, no steam equivalent springing readily to mind! The corporate blue of the Deltic and its train now appears what it is – from a different age to today's jumble of liveries, much of what is not far short of official travelling graffiti, a complaint from which I readily exclude the smart GNER successor. The tracks on the right are the old Midland line connecting Peterborough with Leicester/ Nottingham via Stamford, Manton Junction, Oakham and Melton Mowbray.

The perils of having a friend who was *nearly* in the know! In the early 1960s pre-electrification work in the Northampton area dictated frequent mid-week main line diversions. On Thursday 27 February 1964 the grapevine confidently forecast a special Euston to Liverpool boat train, rostered for no less than a Coronation, at a time when they might not be around the next day. This was too good an opportunity to ignore and a foolproof ploy akin to truancy from work was carefully organised. So far, so good. What actually turned up at Duston West at 11am on Thursday 27 February 1964 was Stanier Class 5 44862 of Rugby on a down freight. A number of modern phrases describing our thoughts come to mind, as did the perils of waiting much longer just in case... Hunsbury Hill tunnel mouth can be seen just beyond the overbridge at the rear of the train.

Lunchtime on Saturday 22 September 1962, and I had just finished work, but was unable to resist calling at base. Also finished work for the weekend were Stanier 8F 2-8-0s 48686 of 2B Nuneaton and our own 48422. They are heading along the line of Northampton's first public railway, that from Blisworth to Peterborough, en route to the shed, some 300 yards behind the camera. Once alongside the shed, they would reverse at Bridge Street junction, first call the coaling plant. On the 'last in, first out' basis, it would be very likely that 48686 and 48422 could have found themsleves on electrification special trains the following day.

Friday 13 March 1964 was not a day to trifle with, but it did produce a lunchtime shot of Stanier 2-8-0 48132 of Wellingborough, taking the Peterborough to Blisworth section with iron ore from Irthlingborough, via Bletchley and Oxford to Ebbw Vale steelworks. A victim of the September 1963 shed code changes, Wellingborough, 15A throughout the later LMS and its BR regime successor, slipped down the ratings to 15B, with Kettering moving down to 15C. Why? Merely to reflect Leicester's probably rightful position as the districts 'A' shed. I imagine I was not alone in thinking that it hardly mattered by then.

One of the earliest 8Fs, 48005, which had spent most of its time allocated to the Midland Division, was not actually that far from home when it was photographed running light northwards at Didcot towards Oxford in August 1964. It had moved from Rowsley to Woodford Halse during the summer of 1963 and was probably not particularly unusual at Didcot on inter-regional freight jobs. Its very clean condition was doubtless owed to a recent works visit. It was never fitted with AWS gear, but the cabside star marks it out as one of the relatively few 8Fs which had their driving wheels properly balanced for higher speed trains, while offering a little more comfort to their crews. Photograph Jack Kirke, The Transport Treasury.

Immaculate 6952 KIMBERLEY HALL rests on Didcot shed in August 1964. Its condition contrasts strongly with the images most enthusiasts will recall of the surviving WR engines by that time. The apparent lack of the all embracing electrification flashes, which seemed to be put on anything with wheels is a little odd – 6952 could have actually stood a chance of getting under the wires at Crewe. Parochialism dictated that on seeing a Hall, it was necessary to squint, so that with faith it was possible to convert the image to a Jubilee... Photograph Jack Kirke, The Transport Treasury.

I can never remember when the track in the shed yard at Northampton was in any other condition than that underneath Black 5 45064, photographed on Sunday 8 March 1964. That there was still a little life left in the place was evidenced by the presence of visitors from, if not afar, far enough to be interesting – 45044 of Chester, 45003 of Stoke, 92151 of Saltley (which brought the beloved 2E shedplate back to us) and, from Crewe North, double chimney 44765, with one of our first sightings since the mid-1950s of a real BLACK Black 5, 44762, ex-works and unlined and at the time, a novelty. Even diverted main line parcels trains produced Pacifics 46228 and 46254, and all was well with the world ... wasn't it?

An Oxley-based engine at Northampton shed was generally considered to be a joke. We failed to appreciate that a Western Region shed had any right to run 'one of ours' even if Oxley now found itself operating, coded 2B, under the thumb of Tyseley, which had been given the hallowed 2A code of Rugby. Joke or otherwise, 44841, in reasonably presentable unlined black, was one of the few inhabitants of the shed spared from weekend pre-electrification working. 44841, since the inception of the AWS system on BR, had been allocated on lines not so provided, and therefore did not receive the equipment. This picture was taken a little late in the day at Northampton, 18 April 1965.

By the early 1960s nerves were jangling on both sides of the BR management/workforce divide and insensitive treatment by the BTC of the mass redundancies likely as a part of the modernisation plan led to the first stoppage of trains since the 1955 partial footplate strike. Consequently Wednesday 3 October 1962 was the chosen day, providing the novelty of free, unhindered access to Northampton Castle station in the midday break. This is the almost deserted forecourt, with some non-striking members of the station workforce. The whole of the station frontage, dating from 1881, has that tired and uninviting look which was to be swept away, along with countless jobs, in the rapidly gathering momentum of the modernisation plan. The actual entrance, via the ticket office, was between the Blackpool poster and the rear of the motor cycle. Once inside, the surroundings were equally as drab and uninviting. Sometime in the mid-1960s BR dropped the 'Castle' from the title, though no one, to this day, even newcomers, and much semi-official non-railway literature, refers to the premises as anything other than Castle Station – long may it remain so!

Neither before nor since; Northampton Castle station looking south. Platform 1 is on the left with the main canopy at the far (town) end, with the passenger footbridge in its traditional position hard up against West Bridge. Above the footbridge are the signals controlling the two up lines. Both the left-hand home and (fixed) distant, which controls the platform line, and the right-hand home signal (controlling the up through line) allowed trains to travel straight ahead, to Duston Junction North or to the right, to Roade. After passing Northampton No.1 signalbox, Duston North was the northern point of the triangle, bounded by Duston Junction West and Bridge Street Junction, in which was enclosed the locomotive shed. To the left of the up platform is a parcels train, stranded (this was the occasion of the one day partial strike, Wednesday 3 October 1962) in the bay which had originally served trains for Market Harborough and the Midland Division, as well as the GNR/LNWR Joint line to Nottingham. To the right is the deserted platform 6; with another track to its right it was, in effect, the down slow line of the Northampton loop.

The centre of the up through line at the north end of 'Castle'. The position was almost the length of platform 1 further north, facing north towards Spencer Bridge compared with the previous picture. Northampton No.2 box is to the right, in front of the bridge. From left to right are the two (unseen) down goods lines, a line running out of the northbound bay, the down through line now clear of the end of platform 6 and the two up lines. Note the crossovers just beyond the box, necessary for down freights calling at the extensive goods station, which was to the right, out of the picture. Spencer Bridge has the first signs of attention from the modernisers, who eventually managed to lift it to take the wires and then proceeded to double its road width to take the ever-increasing number of vehicles. Today, only those with long memories would be able to identify the changes at road level.

This view shows the main platform 1, used almost exclusively for services to Euston. With parcels and tail lamps on the platform, the scene could have been between trains on a normal day. A British Transport policeman can be seen further down platform in conversation with clerical staff who normally worked from one of those mysterious behind the scenes offices on the platform. He was, luckily, completely at ease with a be-suited teenager roaming at will around the premises, including the running lines, camera at the ready. From left to right, the lines are the down main or fast along platform six; then comes the up through line, used almost exclusively by the never-ending freights and the up slow line alongside platform one. It would be true to say that any record of a passenger train on the up through line would have been a main line diversion – an event for which most local enthusiasts lived in hope!

Thanks to an understanding boss, and an early example of what is nowadays called flexi-time, the slightly late departure of the Llandudno-Euston semi-fast on Tuesday 10 March 1964 was not overly important, Britannia Pacific 70020 MERCURY, then one of Willesden's finest, providing the power. 70020 has just left the southbound platform 1, and passed under West Bridge, which can be seen to have no parapet other than a wire fence. It was being lifted for the forthcoming electrification and widened slightly in a welcome piece of official planning co-operation. Another visible example of the pleasures to come is the electricity sub-station, built in the new, blue brick style of the period on the down side. Unfortunately, the long standing LNWR water tank towering over the impostor was not to stand for much longer. The River Nene (properly pronounced Nen) was diverted from its natural course when the station was built in 1880-81. It runs under the lines from the up side to the down side immediately south of Spencer Bridge, and returns under the lines beyond the southern end of the station's now-removed south bays, south of West Bridge before heading for East Anglia and the Wash.

The down Royal Scot, diverted via the Northampton Loop on Sunday 16 September 1962, headed by Type 4 diesel D308, had rather more interest at the rear. The full height rear board of the Royal Scot was always a colourful sight and in view of what was disappearing before our eyes, it was felt that it was only a matter of time before it was no more. Sadly, it was, or rather wasn't. Other expresses provided with similar tailboards were The Red Rose, The Mid-Day Scot and, in later years, The Caledonian. Note the 'double peg' watching over D308's progress past Duston West box. Normally standard fare was worthy only of a 'single peg' with only diverted main line trains invested with the prestige of a 'double peg'. The anticipation created by an unexpected 'double peg down' at Duston West automatically brought all other non-railway pursuits to a halt for the duration, even if it did not produce whatever we had hoped for.

Dieselisation brought this one time Polmadie Britannia to Crewe North, via a spell at Leeds Holbeck and it was a very welcome, even surprising visitor in our back garden on Sunday 30 September 1962. 70053 MORAY FIRTH was in attendance with the p-way men working on the 15 arches viaduct and the Pacific's immaculate condition was quite a tonic. In eleven short years, the Britannias had moved full circle. When new, given the right conditions they could all (given a level of attention to the lineside bordering on the pathological) have been seen running in from Crewe works on Western Division expresses. By the end of 1963 all 55 were to be found on the Western Division (which by then effectively included Kingmoor). The realisation that such far off exotica as FLYING DUTCHMAN, RISING STAR, ROBIN HOOD and the like were turning up at Northampton as often as CHARLES DICKENS, TENNYSON and BYRON had in earlier years was, if somewhat startling, nevertheless greatly appreciated.

Even though by Friday 13 March 1964, Jubilee 45590 TRAVANCORE belonged to Warrington, rather than its former Midland shed at Millhouses and was no longer likely to be found heading expresses, it was still very presentable. Brought to a halt at Duston West with a down freight, its elegant lines demanded recording. For many years a feature of the Western Division in our area had been the group of northbound 'fitted' freights which passed Blisworth or travelled via (possibly calling at) Northampton, during weekday afternoons. We used to marvel at how it was possible for everything behind the loco, tender included, to be heading in different directions at differing speeds, with the crews of the Class 5, unrebuilt Patriot or Jubilee seemingly indifferent to the spectacle. LMS 6P 4-6-0s were not uncommon on fitted freights, but the first few occasions that rebuilt Royal Scots, rebuilt Patriots and Britannias found themselves in such straitened circumstances created a well-founded air of apprehension that was never to leave us.

The driver of 6871 BOURTON GRANGE looks to be making ready to move off from Basingstoke WR station, with what appears to be a shunting movement judging from the position of the pointwork and the shunt signal in the 'off' position. Photograph Jack Kirke, The Transport Treasury.

Western Region 43XX 2-6-0 6385 heads back to the Western Region with a short train, carrying express headlamps, near Betchworth during August 1962. Habitués of the area will doubtless know to what train the reporting number V86 refers. By that date, the letter V usually referred to a train heading into the Western Region from elsewhere, but the ensemble does not have the appearance of a long distance train, unless it was to be joined further along the line. 6385 would have probably started its journey from Redhill on the old SECR, running onto the former LSWR at Shalford Junction and onto Guildford and back to the sanctuary of its home region. Photograph Jack Kirke, The Transport Treasury.

I was under no illusion that Friday 1 January 1965 would be the last New Year's Day that steam would be seen on shed at Northampton. Unfortunately, conditions for photography were unsuitable overnight as the old year turned into the new one, but the following night was a clear, frosty one, and I just had to attempt to record what it had been like when we wandered around the shed in the hours of darkness over the preceding few years. This was the scene at 9.00pm that evening, leaning stiffly against a fence on the far side of the then, and not for much longer, freight-only line linking Blisworth with Peterborough via Wellingborough London Road. The hope was that holding the lens open on a B setting would not produce a blurred image, but just possibly a reasonable picture. This was the result, and from the left can be seen, a red buffer beam on number 1 road, four Stanier locos on roads 3, 4, 5 and 8, and the shed breakdown train in its usual position, taking up all of number 10. In the gloom can be seen the ash plant, the welcoming glow from the coal attendant's 'office', and the coaling plant, under which (the reader may be assured) stands a tender-first Standard Class 5 4-6-0, 73048 of Nuneaton, which had just come onto the shed, still showing the red tail light which had been correct until reversal at Bridge Street Junction signalbox, the lights of whose signals can be seen as splashes of red and orange.

A late afternoon view of Northampton shed and yard, taken from the west, exit end. The locos on view were standard fare for the period, a mix of Stanier Class 5 4-6-0s, 8F 2-8-0s, the odd Stanier 2-6-0, 4F 0-6-0s and local Jinties. We saw all classes of ex-LMS named 4-6-0s from 1959 onwards but strangely, none were present on this occasion, Sunday 30 September 1962. The diesels, D5023 and D5034 peering out from road 10, were shortly to come off shed past the camera, reversing at Duston Junction West, to head for Castle station to take a semi-fast to Euston, via Blisworth at about 6.00pm, by which time the camera should have been put away, as each shot cost in the region of 2/0d (10p). In fact it was not and a presentable diesel shot was surreptitiously canned.

'Round the side'. In its heyday, which was really before my time, locos stabling on Northampton shed used to be found all over the place. During the 1950s and 1960s, the allocation rarely exceeded forty-five and, especially in the 1961-65 period, the need to find power for countless Sunday pre-electrification jobs created plenty of space. Therefore the sight of Standard Class 4 75054 of Bletchley and Britannia 70021 MORNING STAR of Willesden in this open area adjacent to the infrequently used turntable on Sunday 12 April 1964 was noteworthy. The shed's location, inside a triangle, rendered the turntable semi-redundant when the Duston West exit was installed in 1941. The Britannia managed to hold onto its smoke deflector handrails to the end of its time and how much better it looked for it. Find out all about Northampton shed, the canal, hole in the fence and every oily puddle, in *Urchin Tales* in *British Railways Illustrated Summer Special No.6*.

A general view of the shed yard at Northampton on Sunday 6 June 1965. By this date, sixteen short weeks to closure to steam and effectively The End, the number of steam rosters was becoming fewer by the week. Inhabitants that day were few and far between and those visible were all Staniers, 8F 48077 of Bletchley and local Class 5s 45134 and 45392, backed up by visitors 44962 of Saltley and 44887 of Kingmoor. At any earlier period a visitor from Saltley would have been quite unusual – one from Kingmoor would have created near-ecstasy. As it happened, there were few visitors we could have imagined which would have helped dispel the feeling of imminent doom. The only previous Kingmoor visitor I could recollect had been Clan 72005 CLAN MACGREGOR on a memorable evening during September 1955; though less than ten years previously it was seemingly a lifetime away. I may have seen – even missed – one or two Kingmoor visitors but I never managed to sniff out one from Polmadie. That would have induced total ecstasy.

Mid-afternoon on Saturday 19 September 1964 saw 44414, a Leicester 4F 0-6-0, defying the recent prohibition of yellow-striped engines under the electrification wires of the West Coast main line. 44414 was heading a railtour rejoicing under the title 'The Cobbler' whose itinerary obviously covered many routes around the shoe manufacturing county of Northamptonshire. The train must have travelled under the wires from at least Bletchley to Blisworth! Note on the right of the picture, the rear end of an up coal train, which would have come from Nottinghamshire via Market Harborough to Northampton, and then onto the direct route to Roade and the West Coast main line. Although the route taken by 44414 finally closed to all traffic early in 1969, one track was retained for training staff in the use of track care equipment for about one mile behind the camera. This survived until about 1999 before disappearing under the inevitable housing development.

After long agonising, the wanton purchase of a Kodachrome 2 (25ASA) film led me in mid-afternoon on Saturday 22 September 1962 to the old LNWR carriage shed on the up side of the Blisworth route just south of Castle station. As luck had it, instead of the hoped for Stanier Pacific, an EE diesel turned up, but compensation came when two Bedford 4Fs, 43935 and 44171, appeared on a northbound track train. They would doubtless have caused the customary road chaos while the gates at the nearby Bridge Street Level Crossing were closed. In the way of the world, this was superseded by a splendidly expensive modern bridge (midway between Bridge Street crossing and the site of Bridge Street Junction) some years after traffic had been reduced to about one train per week. Brush Type 2 D5623 of March, laying over between jobs on the Peterborough-Northampton service, given a little more luck could have been a B1 or Class 5 4-6-0. During the 1950s we had seen D16s, B12s and the odd B17, and we knew we were scraping the bottom of the barrel by this time.

The view looking south over the parapet of West Bridge, Northampton. This bridge, which carried the A45/A428 road westwards out of town over the railway, actually divided Castle station into two sections. The main part of the station was behind the camera while in front of and to the left were the bay platforms which had served trains to/from Blisworth, Bedford, Wellingborough, Peterborough and even Nottingham. This last service took cascaded Western Division heavies such as Patriots, Scots and Britannias onto the branch (as we saw it) to Wellingborough from the time of the diesel invasion of 1959/60 onwards until closure. The LNWR carriage shed stands in the left distance, with the Rugby-Northampton-Roade loop diverging right onto its 1 in 200 climb through Hunsbury Hill tunnel. Activity can be just seen in the clouds of exhaust emanating from the engine shed in the far middle distance. This morning, Monday 16 March 1964, had conveniently provided a powdering of snow, which proved irresistible.

Castle station on the bitterly cold evening of Friday 1 January 1965. The station is in the throes of modernisation, with the up platform canopy completely removed and that of the down platform 6 not far behind. A string of electric light bulbs festoons the platform, luckily providing far more light than the gas lamps which had survived until a few weeks earlier. The 'overhead' is already in place, as yet unenergised, passing under the new, utilitarian passenger footbridge in the new, healthy, open air style. The ghost-like characters seen on the platform were waiting for the arrival of the 6.55pm Euston to Wolverhampton train, which actually arrived at the platform out of sight to the left. Over the years the passage of this train had been the evening's highlight. Its apotheosis came on successive evenings, Thursday and Friday, 18/19 June 1959, when 45679 ARMADA and 45704 LEVIATHAN, newly, and unknown to us, transferred from Kingmoor to Crewe North, coasted past the astonished masses.

While waiting in the countryside between Duston Junction West and the closed Duston Sidings for a local area railtour (which pleasingly ran with a large 'The Cobbler' headboard) in mid-afternoon, Saturday 22 September 1964, an Irthlingborough to Ebbw Vale iron ore train hove into view behind Stanier 2-8-0 48748 of Derby. We used not to pay much attention to this type of working, accepting without much thought that they would be forever a part of life as we knew it. Only some years later did I discover that when they waited half a mile back along the line, outside the shed premises for what seemed like ages, they were in fact re-crewing as well as possibly waiting for the Blisworth motor to take precedence on its interminable sprints connecting Castle station and the main line stoppers. Visitors from Derby shed were always unusual at Duston West.

What we used to call a record shot, which in my defence, is why I took it. This is one of Rugby's best, 8F 2-8-0 48120, which, if my records had survived intact, would surely have been amongst my top few most frequent sightings. By the spring of 1964 we had ceased inviting BR to scrap too-frequent visitors, but, as was always the case, that much missed organisation failed to listen!

One of the by-products of the huge amount of pre-electrification Sunday work which befell Northampton shed and no doubt all the other sheds in the monster's path, was that there were often gaps left inside the shed which allowed photographic opportunities not available in the days when all the local complement and our many visitors were crammed into the premises. On Sunday 12 April 1964 Crewe North Jubilee 45556 NOVA SCOTIA was parked at the inner end of the slightly shorter Road 1. With Road 2 empty, it afforded the opportunity to experiment. Jubilee 45655 and Britannias 70021 and 70023 were also in residence. They would most probably have been used for northbound freights the next day, as would NOVA SCOTIA. The days when they would have found themselves deputising for unreliable Type 2 or Type 4 diesels on the flood of Euston-bound Monday morning trains had, it has to be admitted, passed by that time. Such a gathering in earlier years would have been unheard of. Until sometime during around late 1959, when the English Electric Type 4 diesels arrived, the presence of even a single 'namer' on the shed would have stirred the masses.

Jubilee 45700 AMETHYST had always held celebrity status among our squad. This was traceable to the period in late 1950/early 1951 when it ran nameless on the arrival of the first BR Pacific 70000, which was bequeathed its name, 'Britannia'. Not that I saw either loco until some years later – 45700 during a short period when it was allocated to Blackpool and 70000 at Norwich, while en route en-famille to Northampton's then east coast playground, Great Yarmouth. 'Cabbing' locos was not one of our main indulgences, so I must assume at this distance, that it was impending doom that had (me at least) photographing this view from the fireman's side. This was on Sunday 5 April 1964 and we were painfully aware that such opportunities were not likely to be available for much longer. We did not, however, expect visits from all the classes of LMS 'namers' to be a thing of the past by September 1 of the same year.

Cigarette in mouth, then almost standard practice, the fireman appears to be trimming the coal at the rear of the tender of rebuilt Merchant Navy Pacific 35020 BIBBY LINE while it awaits the rightaway from Southampton Central with an afternoon Bournemouth to Waterloo express. The date is most likely during a summer prior to 1963, since no electrification warning flashes can be discerned. The fashions exhibited by the watchers on the platform would seem to support a date of 1960, 1961 or 1962. There is a school of thought that tended towards the idea that London Midland Region enthusiasts would have become much more familiar with this neck of the woods if the darkly rumoured notion of exiling the Coronation Pacifics to the Southern Region had come to fruition in 1964. With the benefit of hindsight, and ignoring the practicalities which have since come to light, even they must consider it was pie in the sky. Now, if they had gone onto Glasgow-Aberdeen services... Photograph Dr A. Roscoe, The Transport Treasury.

An up Bournemouth express has recently arrived at Waterloo behind rebuilt West Country 34097 HOLSWORTHY which, by dint of its 70D shedplate, denoting is Eastleigh allocation, can be dated as after the multitude of September 1963 shed code changes. It was, and still is, astonishing to an East Midlander, whose steam world was much diminished after the yellow stripe summer of 1964, that such scenes could still be repeated for almost another four years, the only difference perhaps being that the layers of grime increased in later years and many of the attractive nameplates and scrolls/badges disappeared prematurely. HOLSWORTHY has still has not received the tell-tale electrification warning flashes – the Southern, hardly surprisingly, did not seem over concerned about their application, although the third rail must have had its moments of danger. Did the driver of 34097 really manage to get so close to the hydraulic buffers without apparently compressing them? See how they match those in the adjacent platform. Photograph Dr A. Roscoe, The Transport Treasury.

Kings Cross A4 60003 ANDREW K McCOSH passes Hitchin during June 1962. In the fullness of time, I came to appreciate the flowing grace of this class and although I have only ever seen the preserved MALLARD in full dress, I consider its looks not a patch on the A4s that I saw as they appeared after the full skirt was removed. The Brunswick green livery with black and orange lining bequeathed us by the Great Western well suited the class and I believe, all classes of all Regions similarly coloured. Preserved examples of LNER garter blue and LMS maroon fail to impress me as much as the later post-1948 liveries, although I am the first to acknowledge that we are all of an era and that had I arrived twenty years sooner, I might well take a different viewpoint. My only regret is that on home territory, any livery usually came to be submerged under layers of grime. Even the inspired British Railways maroon, with either BR or LMS style lining, on the Stanier Pacifics soon looked the same from a distance as the green. Photograph Jack Kirke, The Transport Treasury.

Yet another well turned out 'Eastern', A1 60118 ARCHIBALD STURROCK on express duty at Brookmans Park in July 1962. Any non-Gresley Pacific design always appeared to be tolerated, rather than revered, by such of the 'Eastern' masses that I came across, but I would hazard a guess that the A1s were up there with the best of any Region's offerings. Perhaps we will find out the truth when the new 60163 'Tornado' takes to the rails sometime in the not too distant future. Surely when the builders of 60163 have completed their task they will build an original Patriot. Mind you, they might struggle to come up with an original number, so possibly they will move on to a Fowler 2-6-4 tank. Photograph Jack Kirke, The Transport Treasury.

Sunday 27 October 1963 saw an early 9.00am start after the excitement of the previous evening, to 'do' New England shed. Although 35A (34E never happened!) was still then officially in Northamptonshire, going over to the 'Eastern' was the equivalent of journeying to the far reaches of Europe today. Having, unusually, opted for the 'permission to have a look round please' tack, it was duly given by authority in the shape of the Shed Foreman, or was it a cleaner? The bag of A4s was restricted to 60025 FALCON, which was peering out of the shed front, almost unphotographable. Doom and gloom was everywhere, brightened somewhat by the presence of in-service A3s 60106 and 60112. Out of action, probably stored, were numerous examples of A3s, B1s, and V2s, but how could you truly differentiate between official storage, dumped out-of-use for ever, or merely resting up for a few days in those saddening times? In use as a stationary boiler was withdrawn K3 61912. The left-hand side motion of A3 60112 ST SIMON was my only decent effort on a day whose gloom effortlessly despatched Kodachrome 2s 25ASA to the boundary!

Sunday 4 October 1964 produced as cold an easterly wind as I can ever recollect braving in the interests of recording the end of our world. It was also the day on which a Coronation Pacific was due to stamp its superiority on the Great Northern line for the second year running – this time with a Kings Cross to York enthusiasts special. The previous occasion was in the summer of 1963, when 46245 CITY OF LONDON ran a special from Kings Cross to Doncaster and back. Having failed to anticipate the events of September 1964, when the last survivors of the Coronations were withdrawn without ceremony, we journeyed eastwards to record the scene. That early withdrawal of the Stanier Pacifics was the reason for 70020 MERCURY of Willesden shed turning up on the special. Heroes to the end, the call of the home fires was not strong enough to stop us calling in at Kettering shed where, of all things, Low Moor's B1 61016 INYALA was in just the right spot in the yard. Parochialism ruled – it was my only visit to the shed – just sixteen miles from home!

On the afternoon of Sunday 23 September 1962 the regular meat train from, I believe, Holyhead to Broad Street failed to produce any of the unexpected that we had come to expect. Willesden's Class 5 45044 is doing the business at Duston Junction West, Northampton. The engine shed yard was to the left of the ash and coaling plant seen in the right background. The line from Blisworth to Wellingborough and Peterborough passes to the right of the shed. Locos leaving the shed headed towards the camera on the right-hand line and crossed over behind the camera to head for their next duty. On the appropriately named 'top line' the activity is surrounding preparations for the renewal of the bridges over the 'bottom line' and the unseen canal. The attending trains were in the simmering care of Stoke's distinguished Crab 2-6-0 42856 and local visitor 48376 of Kettering. The crane was from Rugby and its efforts ensured that, by mid-November, the noisy old bridges we had come to love were no more. The previous week's meat train had produced the stunning sight of Shrewsbury Jubilee 45682 TRAFALGAR, forever associated with 22A Bristol Barrow Road, where it had been when I last saw it locally some ten years before.